DOCTOR COLORING BOOK (MEDICAL SCHOOL) MIDNIGHT EDITION

CRYSTAL
COLORING BOOKS

ISBN-13: 978-1718848498
ISBN-10: 1718848498

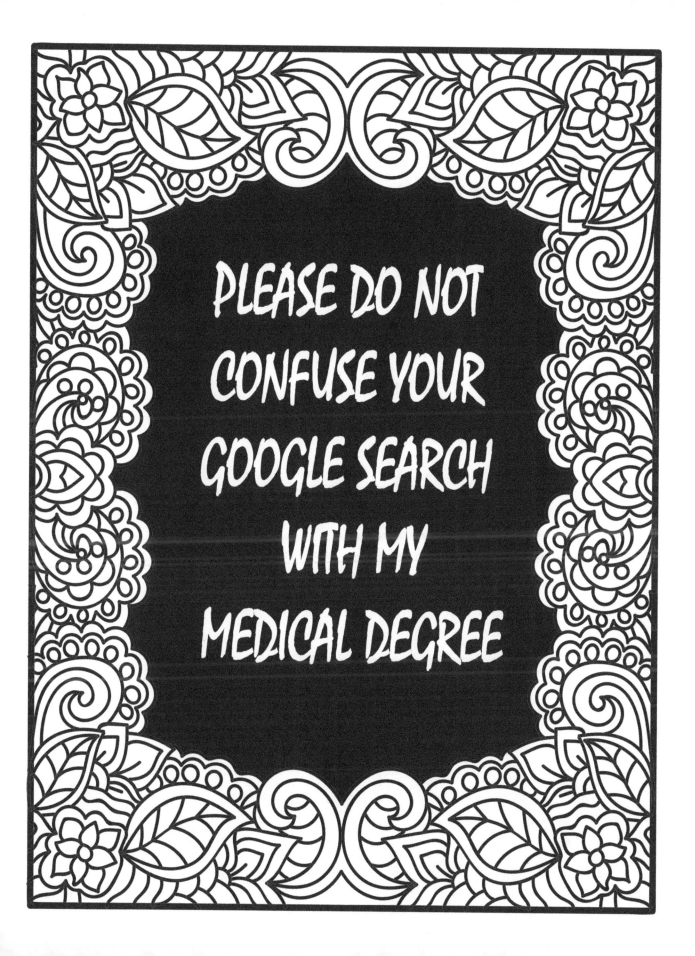

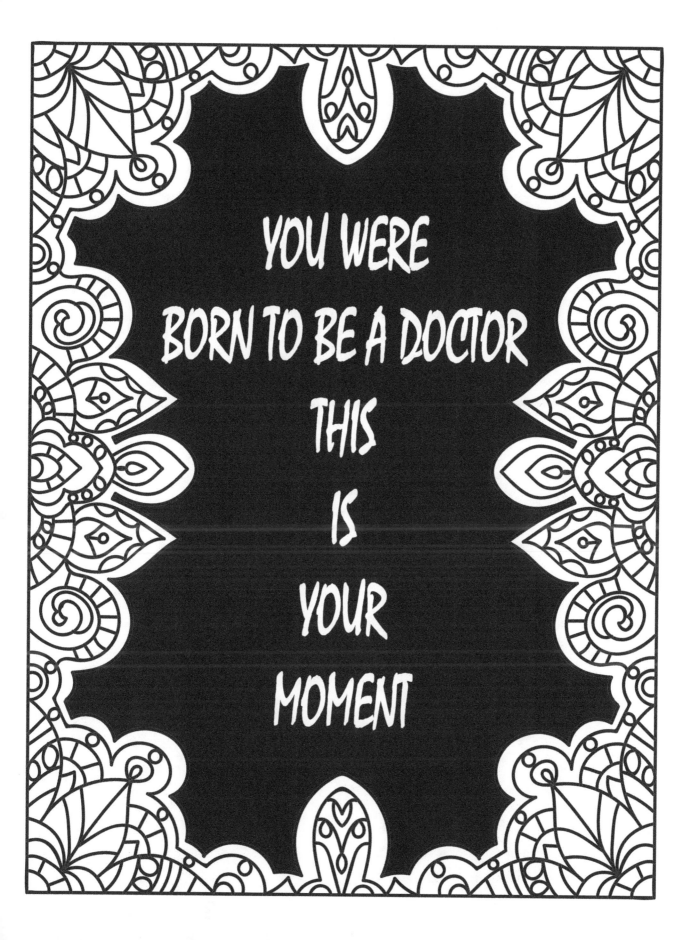

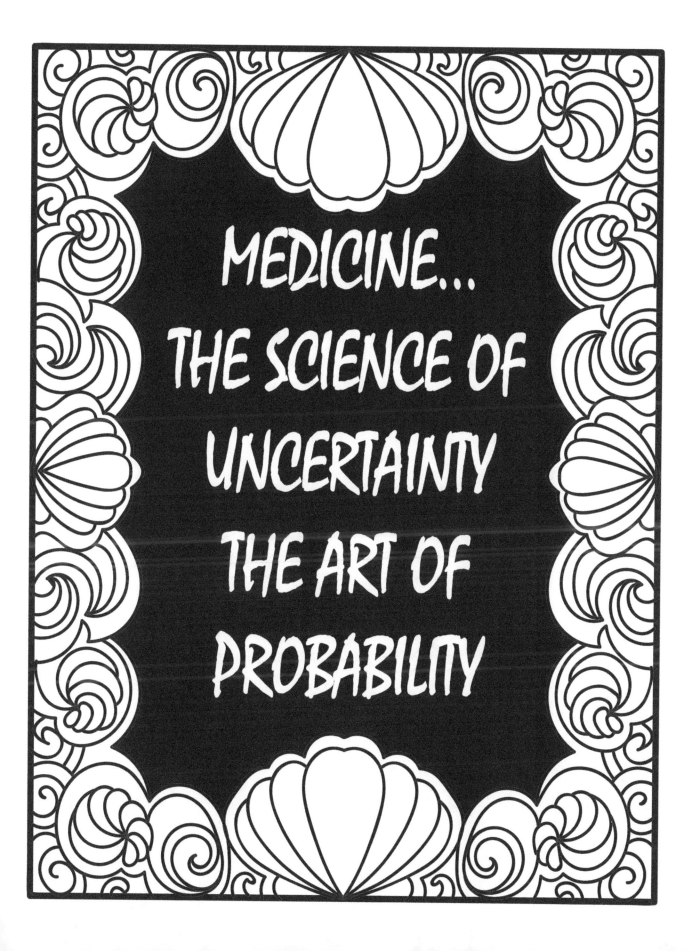

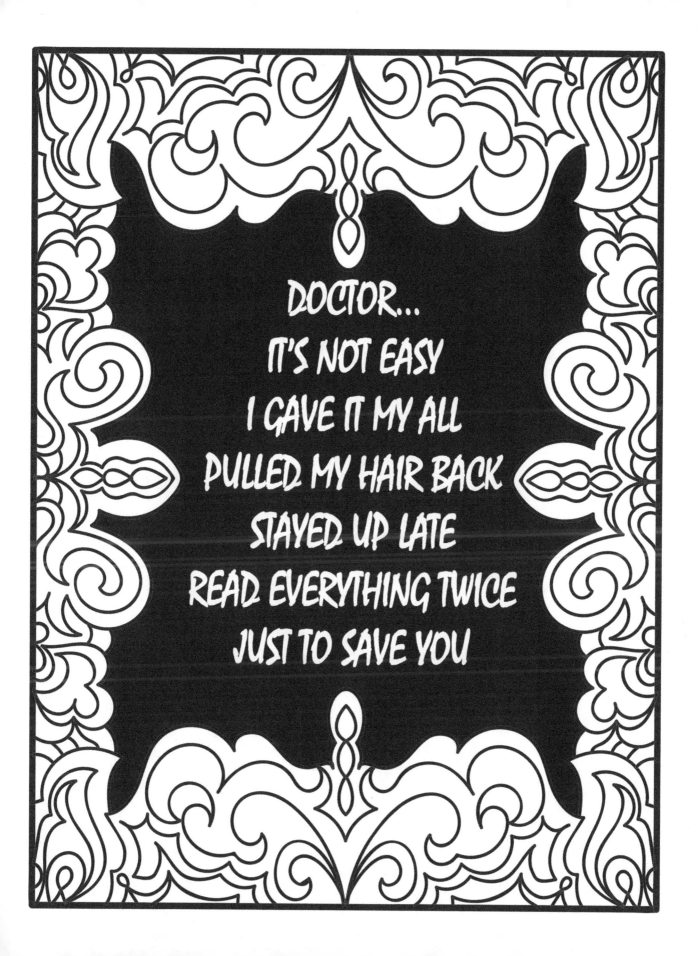

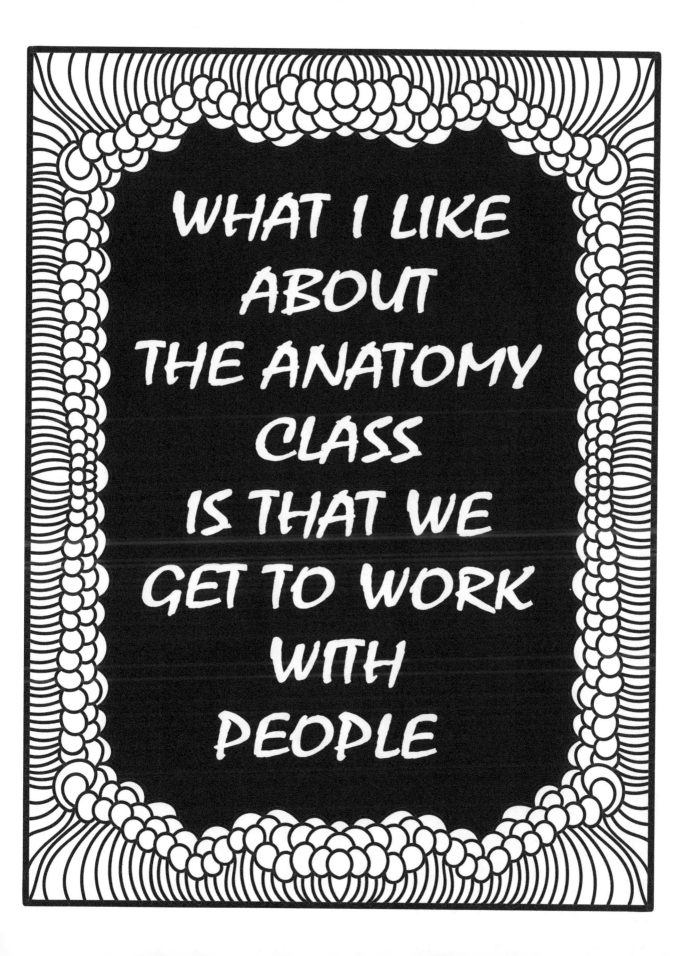

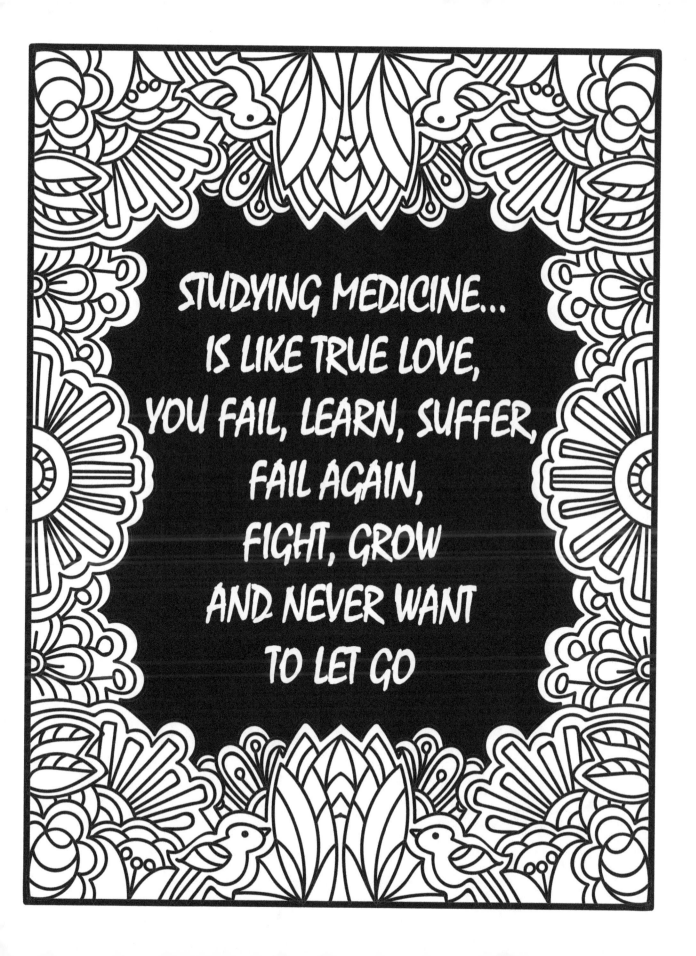

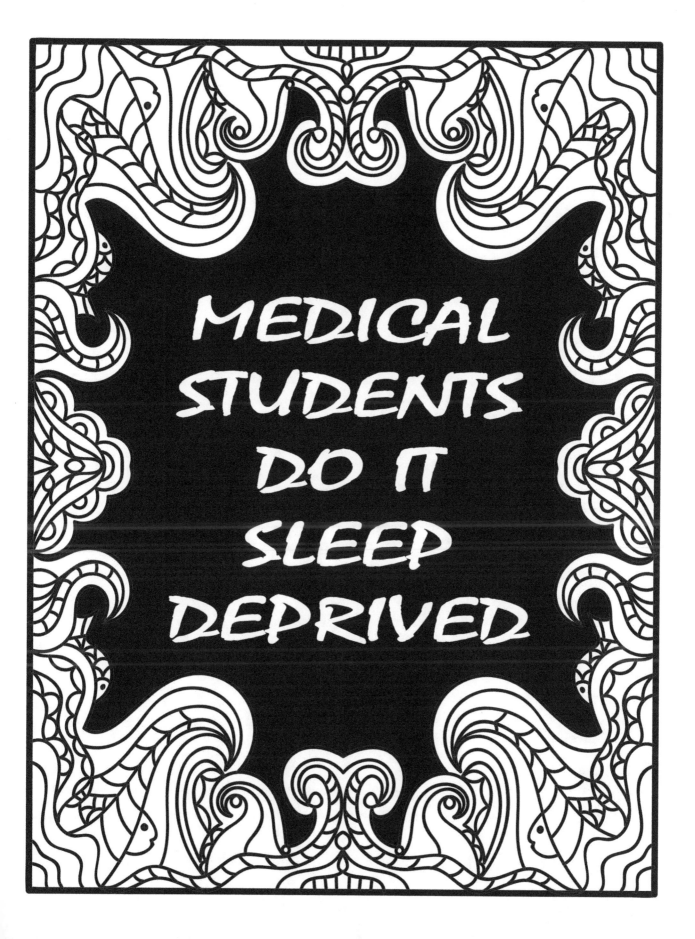

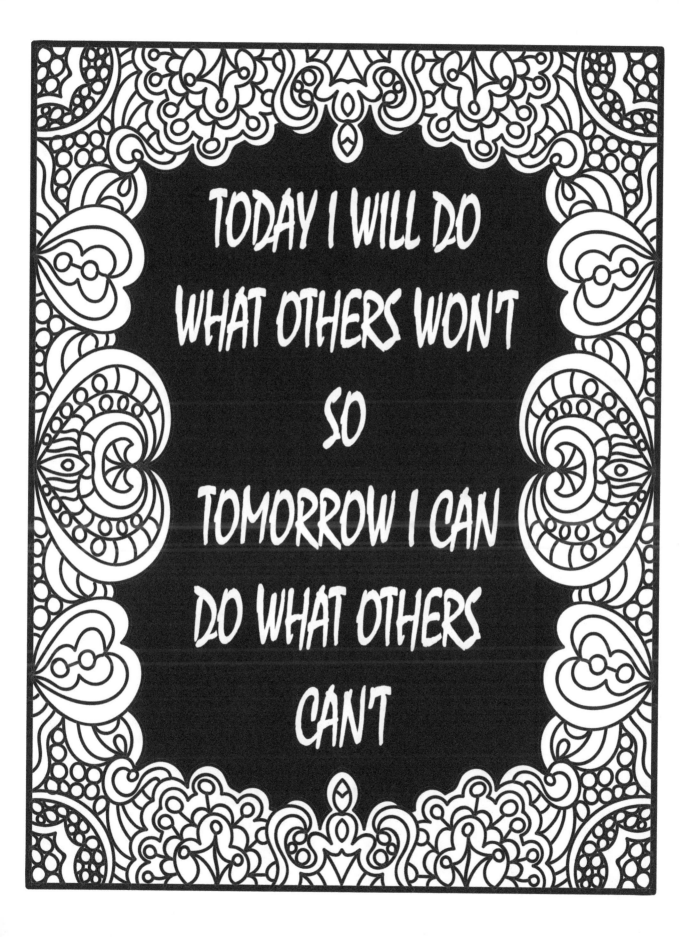

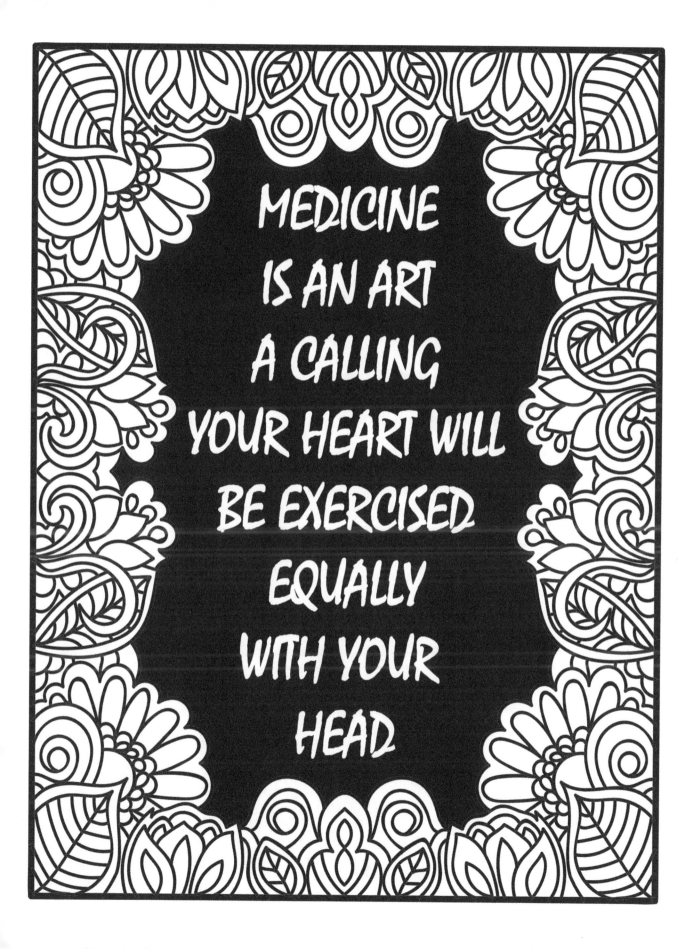

COLOR TEST PAGE

COLOR TEST PAGE

CPSIA information can be obtained
at www.ICGtesting.com
Printed in the USA
BVHW010605191218
535877BV00037B/822/P